WHAT MAKES EARTH SOIL DIFFERENT FROM MARS?

SOIL SCIENCE FOR KIDS

Children's Earth Sciences Books

Speedy Publishing LLC
40 E. Main St. #1156
Newark, DE 19711
www.speedypublishing.com

In this book, we're going to cover how Earth's soil is different from Mars and why it might matter to us in the future. So let's get right to it.

Mars expedition transport, mars rover.

Imagine you're an astronaut and you're stranded on Mars. Could you grow your own food from seeds or from some cuttings? Recent books and movies have posed this question and offered some solutions, but no one really knows for sure because humans have never set foot on Mars.

Our rovers have taken soil samples on Mars and we've analyzed the samples once they were brought back to Earth. These rover samples give us some clues about the soil that's on the Red Planet.

Several layers of soil.

THE COMPLEX SOIL OF EARTH

If you were a Martian and you sent a rover-type vehicle to Earth, you'd have to take a lot of samples to get a feeling for all the different types of soil on Earth. That's because soil is a living thing, and it varies a lot from place to place depending on the types of rocks and minerals, the type of organic matter it contains, and the amount of water present.

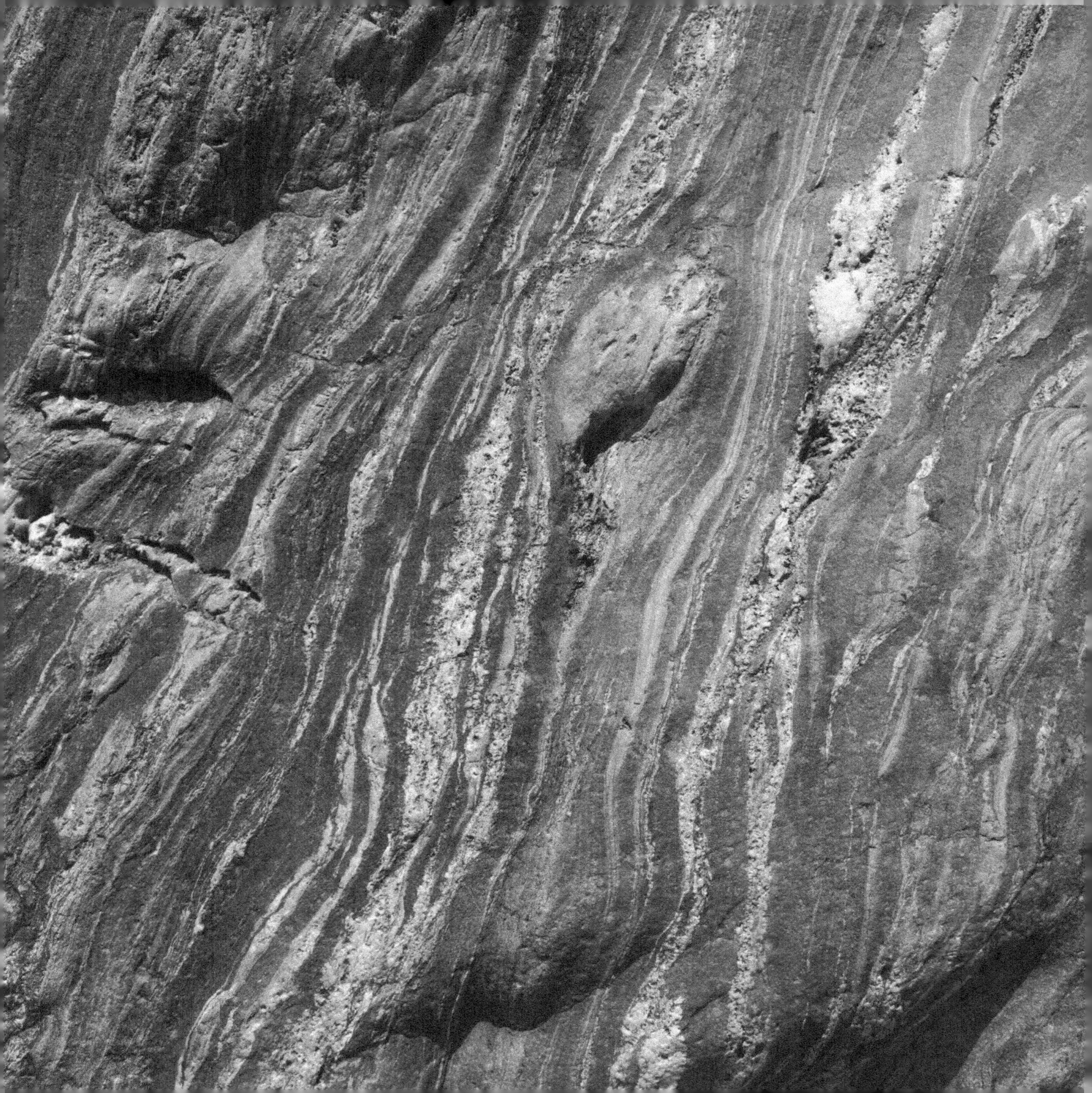

For all we know, the same may be true on Mars. We think we know what the surface of Mars is made of, but there may be some surprises in store for us when we actually get there. For example, it's only been a recent discovery that Mars does have some water that flows on its surface. It doesn't have the oceans and waterways of Earth, but any water is better than none at all when it comes to sustaining life. There are ice deposits located there that if melted would have as much water as Lake Superior.

When you go out in your backyard and pick up a handful of dirt, it looks rather ordinary, but the truth is that the soil we have on Earth is a complex mixture that has come about over millions of years. In fact, the process still happens today. When volcanoes push up from the ocean bed to create new islands, it takes thousands of years until the volcanic rock that's there has a topsoil layer on it.

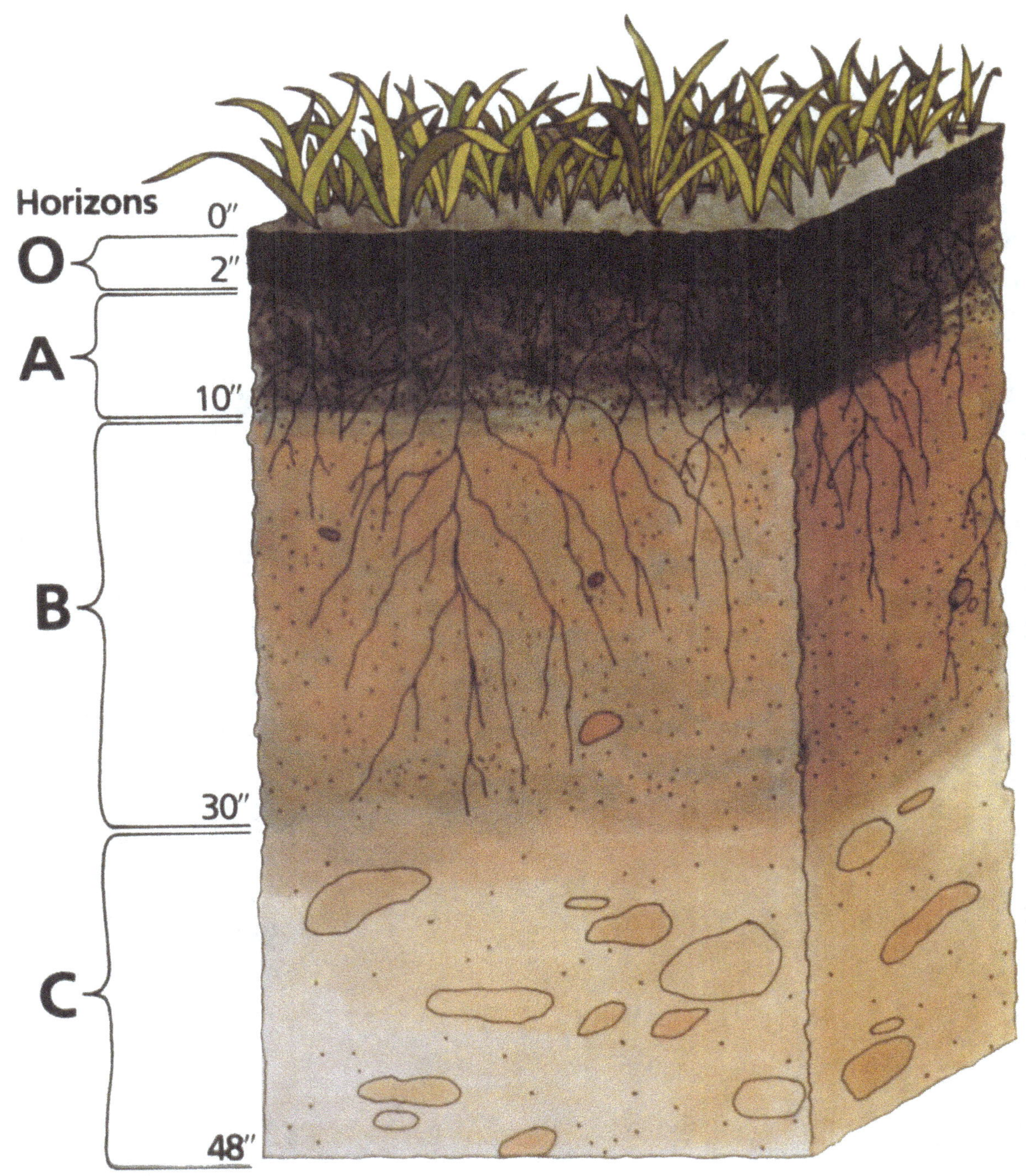

Horizons
0"
O
2"
A
10"
B
30"
C
48"

The upper layer of earth in which plants grow,
a black or dark brown material.

HOW DOES SOIL FORM ON EARTH?

The formation of soil is a complex process when you begin with an area that just has volcanic, metamorphic, or sedimentary rock. Today on Earth we can actually see the beginning stages of this process on islands that have been newly created by volcanoes in Iceland and also in the Pacific Ocean. In the case of lava as soon as it cools down sufficiently, migratory birds, airborne insects, and plant seeds get there rather quickly.

Some plants, like lichens and some mosses, grow rather well on bare rock and this is the start of the soil. Once these plants and animals die the cycle of decomposition starts and this is what transforms organic matter into the topsoil. Weather cycles will cause breakdown of the rocky surface.

After thousands of years of interactions between plants, animals, weather, water, and decomposers, the upper layers of the volcanic rock will have soil of different types.

New life emerging out of the soil.

EARTH HAS LIVING SOIL

Soil on Earth is a very complicated mixture. It contains minerals and fragments of rocks as well as air and water. It also contains decomposing organic matter. Mixed in with all this inanimate matter are billions of organisms from microscopic bacteria to creatures as large as burrowing mammals.

Just like bedrock has layers that give us the details of Earth's past, the layers in soil tell a lot about the history of the source and the area that surrounds it. Soil scientists call these layers the soil horizons.

- **Horizon O:** This layer is made of organic matter, such as leaves that are decomposing. This horizon is very thin in some soils, quite thick in others, and not present at all in some soils.

- **Horizon A:** This layer is called the topsoil. It's made of minerals from the parent rocks that lie below mixed with decomposing organic matter. This is one of the layers where plants and organisms of all types thrive.

- **Horizon E:** This is called the eluviated horizon. This layer has bits of clay, fragments of minerals, organic matter, both decomposing materials and living organisms, granules of sand and silt particles of resistant rocks, such as quartz. Not all soils have this layer, but older soils and some forest soils do.

- **Horizon B:** This layer, called the subsoil, is filled with minerals that have moved down from horizons A and E and accumulated.

- **Horizon C:** This is the layer at the Earth's surface where the soil came from.

- **Horizon R:** This is the mass of rock, like granite, basalt, sandstone, or limestone that is the parent material that produces soil. However, it needs to be exposed to the weather for the rock erosion necessary for soil formation to begin.

Amazing sandstone formations in famous Antelope Canyon at Lake Powell, American Southwest, Arizona, USA

Soil on Earth is absolutely teeming with life. It's filled with bacteria, fungi, algae, protozoa, and nematodes at the microscopic level. All of these microorganisms have an impact on the decomposing of matter and also for the process of changing nitrogen into a usable form for plants.

The limestone mountains.

Curiosity's Color View of Martian Dune After Crossing It.

MARS SOIL

As you can see, the Earth's soil is made up of many different components. The top surface of Mars doesn't have the same kind of soil that Earth does. The most obvious difference is that it doesn't have any living organisms, or at least that's what we currently believe. The surface of Mars is covered with huge expanses of sand and very fine dust. The dust on Mars is so fine that it gives the sky there a reddish color. If you've ever seen copper-reddish rust on a tool or piece of machinery left outdoors, then you have a clue as to how the materials on the surface of Mars look.

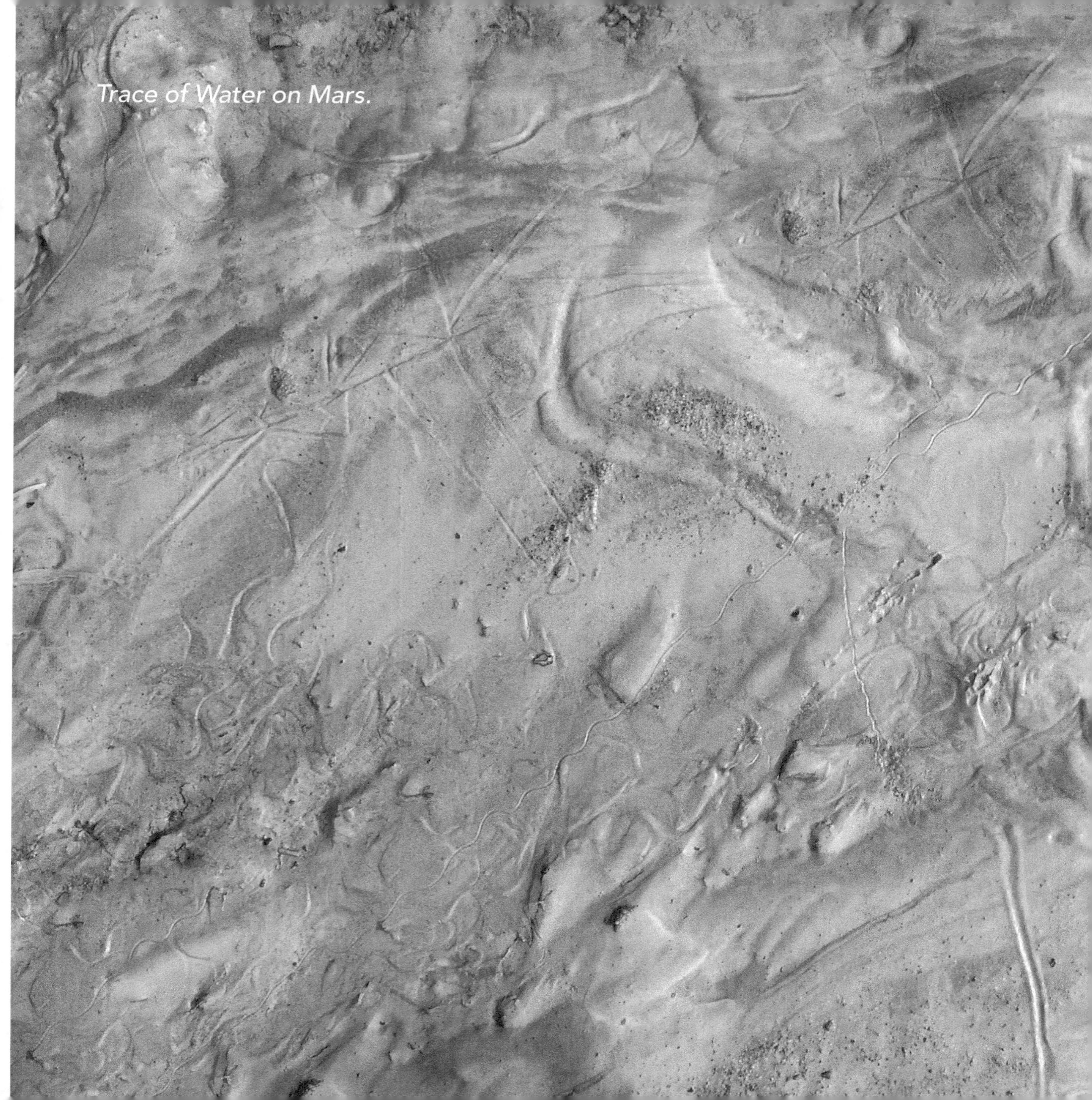
Trace of Water on Mars.

HOW DO WE KNOW ABOUT MARS SOIL?

Although no astronauts have ever stood on the surface of Mars, rovers and other vehicles have landed there and taken soil samples. In June 2008, data from the Phoenix Lander showed that the soil there does contain minerals that are necessary for plant growth, such as sodium, potassium, and chloride. The soil samples were slightly alkaline, which simply means that it has a rather poor soil structure.

MARS

Later that same year, the Lander did some simple experiments by mixing Earth water with soil from Mars. Traces of salt perchlorate were found, which meant that the soil was more complex in structure than originally thought.

On Earth, microorganisms use percholate as a source of energy. When there's an excess of percholate in drinking water here on Earth, a clean-up technique is to introduce microbes. The problem is that in large quantities salt percholate is toxic to humans. Scientists are currently coming up with ideas for how to solve that problem.

In December 2012, the Curiosity rover performed a more thorough analysis of the soil on the red planet, and the samples contained molecules of water as well as other organic compounds, chlorine, and sulphur. There's always the risk that samples have been contaminated by the presence of Earth materials on the vehicles sent into space so scientists are generally very cautious when reporting their data.

There is water in the soil on Mars, but the soil has to be heated up in order for the ice present to change to liquid water. Due to the salt percholate, that water is very, very salty. It's much more salty than any water on Earth. Mars has tons of fresh water at its polar caps so this may eventually prove to be the best source of water for future gardens on Mars. This water would still be exposed to the salts and would have to be desalinated.

Second Phoenix Martian soil scoop.

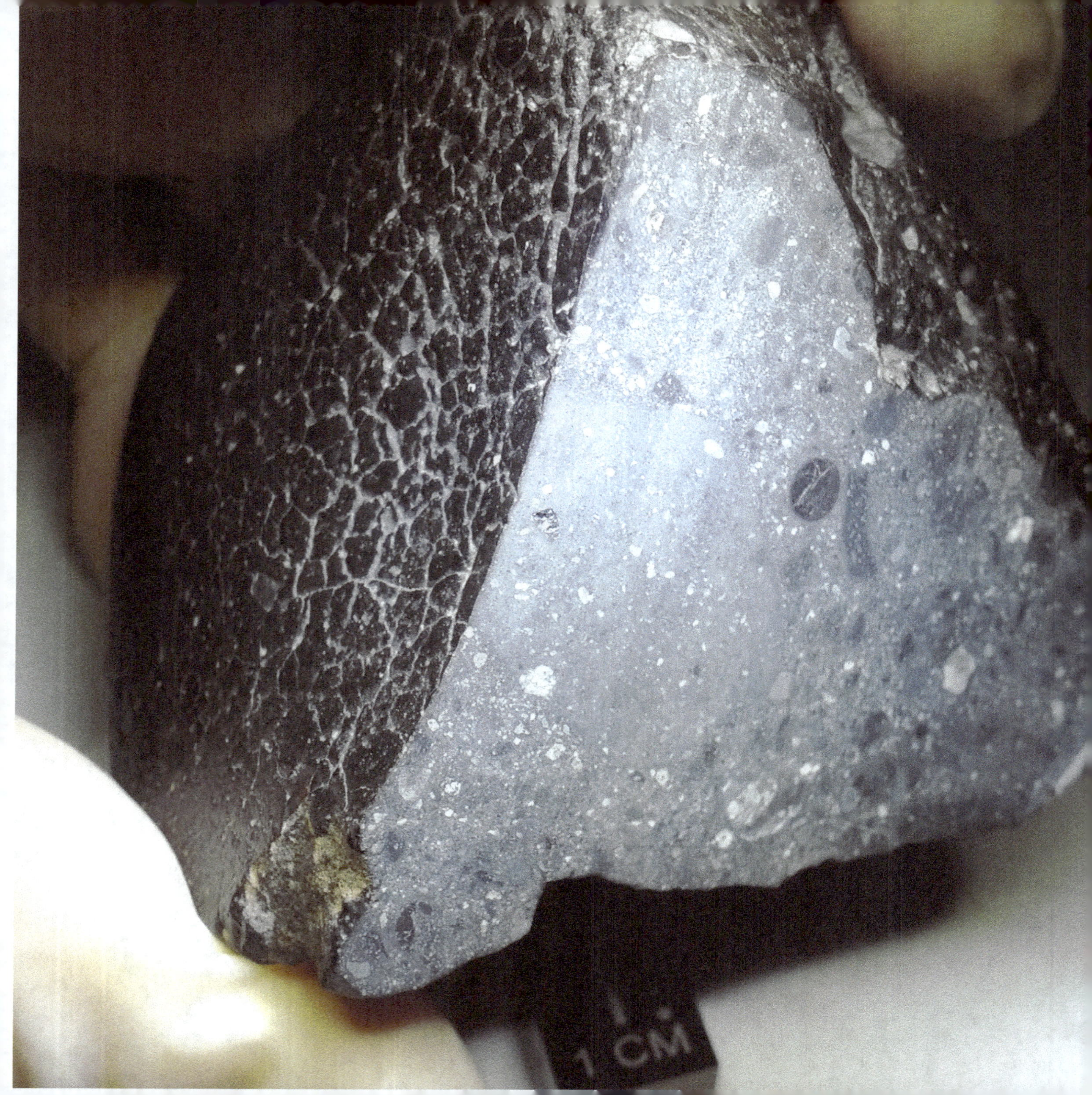
1 CM

The other problem with growing plants on Mars is that its atmosphere is 100 times thinner that Earth and consists mostly of carbon dioxide. There's not enough oxygen to sustain life. The average temperature is about minus 80 degrees Fahrenheit, but it varies from minus 195 degrees to a very comfortable 70 degrees at its equator at times of the year.

Mars Meteorite - NWA 7034.

Black soil in hand.

FOOD EXPERIMENTS

In 2016, scientists in the Netherlands did experiments to show that crops could be grown on Mars. They grew radishes, peas, and tomatoes and they were edible! They were worried that the plants would take on too many heavy metals from the simulated Mars soil they created. For the most part, the plants didn't absorb those metals, but no one knows how well they would do under the lower gravity conditions on Mars.

Mars rover. Elements of this image furnished by NASA.

TERRAFORMING ON MARS

Scientists have spent a great deal of time discussing terraforming and its been talked about both in science fiction as well as in actual science. The idea is that a planet similar to ours could be shaped by human intervention to make it more like our own planet.

In our solar system, the only planet that comes close to ours in general composition and also in distance to the sun, is Mars. Many different ways have been proposed for warming up the planet and ensuring that its soil and air can support life.

Awesome! Now you know more about why Mars has different soil than Earth and why this will make a difference to future expeditions to Mars. You can find more Earth Science books from Baby Professor by searching the website of your favorite book retailer.

Visit

BABY PROFESSOR
EDUCATION KIDS

www.BabyProfessorBooks.com
to download Free Baby Professor eBooks
and view our catalog of new and exciting
Children's Books